It's all about…

TOUGH TRACTORS

KINGFISHER

First published 2016 by Kingfisher
An imprint of Macmillan Children's Books
20 New Wharf Road, London N1 9RR
Associated companies throughout the world
www.panmacmillan.com

Series editor: Sarah Snashall
Series design: Anthony Hannant (LittleRedAnt)
Adapted from an original text by Hannah Wilson

ISBN 978-0-7534-3939-5

9 8 7 6 5 4 3 2 1

1TR/1115/WKT/UG/128MA

A CIP catalogue record for this book is available from the British Library.

Printed in China

Picture credits
The Publisher would like to thank the following for permission to reproduce their material.
Top = t; Bottom = b; Centre = c; Left = l; Right = r
Front cover, p1 Shutterstock/smereka; Back cover Shutterstock/Smileus; Pages 2-3, 15b,
30-31 Shutterstock/AFNR; 4 AGCO Corp; 5 Shutterstock/Natalya Prokopenko; 5t Shutterstock/
vevchic; 6 Shutterstock/Jeff Dalton; 7 Getty/Science and Society Picture Library; 8-9 CLAAS
KGaA mbH; 8b Shutterstock/chiqui; 9t Shutterstock/tanger; 10, 11t Shutterstock/BasPhoto;
11b Shutterstock/Pierre-Jean Durieu; 12-13, 17b Shutterstock/smereka; 13t Shutterstock/
Stockr; 14 New Holland Agriculture Ltd; 15t Shutterstock/abdulrazak; 16 Shutterstock/
papa1266; 17t Shutterstock/Kletr; 18-19 Shutterstock/B Franklin; 19t Shutterstock/Dmitry
Kalinovsky; 20-21 Alamy/HotShots; 21t Getty/Ofer Zidron/Stocktrek Images; 22-23 CNH
Industrial America LLC; 22b Nokian Heavy Tyres Ltd/Jarkko Puikkonen; 24 ASIrobots;
25t Pforzheim University/Chrisoph Proessler; 25b Valtra Inc; 26-27 Alamy/Simon Perkin;
26b Getty/National Geographic/Jack Fletcher; 28-29 Alamy/picturesbyrob; 32 Shutterstock/
Photobac.
Cards: Front tl AGCO Corp; tr SAME DEUTZ-FAHR GROUP SpA; bl Tomy36; br CNH Industrial
America LLC; Back tl J C Bamford Excavators Ltd; tr CLAAS KGaA mbH; bl Husqvarna Group; br
Deere & Company.

Front cover: Case IH 7220 tractor pulling a trailer for a combine harvester.

CONTENTS

What is a tractor?

A tractor is a very strong vehicle with huge tyres. Tractors are not fast but they can drive over the bumpiest, muddiest or snowiest ground. They can push rocks or pull the heaviest trailers.

In 2014, Manon Ossevoort drove her Massey Ferguson tractor to the South Pole.

FACT...

The power of a tractor's engine is measured in horsepower (hp); 1 hp is the strength of one horse.

A tractor is the most important vehicle on a farm.

SPOTLIGHT: John Deere 9R series

Famous for:	one of the best-selling tractors
Built by:	John Deere
Built:	2011
Engine power:	up to 670 horsepower

The first tractors

The earliest tractors were steam traction engines that were designed to replace horses. They looked a bit like trains and ran on coal. The first diesel tractors were built in the 1920s.

The first tractors were powered by steam engines.

Famous for:	first light farm tractor
Built by:	Daniel Albone
Built:	1901
Engine power:	8 horsepower

The Ivel Agricultural Motor was a very successful early tractor.

Big and tough

Tractors are big strong machines. They have huge wheels to grip the ground. A large diesel engine gives the tractor the power to pull heavy equipment over bumpy surfaces.

Tyres have deep treads to grip mud.

The hydraulic hitch raises and lowers attachments.

The power take-off provides power to the attachments.

The drawbar links to the tractor attachments.

This tractor has an extra set of wheels to give it more grip.

The high cab with glass sides allows the farmer to see clearly.

The powerful diesel engine is good at pulling heavy machines.

The smaller front wheels help steer the tractor.

A weight on the front stops the tractor tipping backwards.

Ploughing work

Farmers who grow crops use different machines that attach to the back of their tractor. To prepare a field for planting, a farmer will use a plough to create a trench of fresh earth called a furrow.

A plough cuts the soil and turns it over to bury the old crops and weeds.

Ploughing competitions test who can plough the neatest and straightest furrows.

FACT...

The first ploughs were pulled by oxen. Many farmers across the world still use oxen to pull their ploughs.

Planting and spraying

When the time is right for planting, the farmer attaches a seed drill to the back of the tractor. The seed drill uses tubes and drills to plant and cover seeds evenly across the field.

A sprayer attachment sprays crops with fertilizer or insecticide.

FACT...

Over 2000 years ago, farmers in ancient Babylon (modern Iraq) used a simple seed drill.

Farmers using a seed drill grow more plants and can have up to eight times more produce to sell.

Combine harvesters

If your field is seven kilometres long, you will need a big machine to harvest it – this machine is a combine harvester. A combine cuts down cereal crops and separates the grain from the stalks.

SPOTLIGHT: New Holland CR10.90

Famous for:	most powerful combine harvester
Built by:	New Holland
Built:	2014
Engine power:	652 horsepower

A tractor pulling a trailer collects the grain from the combine harvester.

A hay baler gathers up the stalks.

A fleet of combine harvesters is needed to harvest vast soybean fields in Brazil.

Other jobs

Tractors are not just great at pulling – they are good at lifting and pushing too. This makes them useful for clearing and building. Bulldozers with huge buckets can move rocks and break down walls. Excavators can dig out the hardest rock and concrete.

A bulldozer is a tractor with a large bucket in the front.

A tractor with a strong grapple on its long arm is used to clear trees.

An excavator with a bucket on a long arm is used for digging.

Backhoe loaders

The most useful tractor for the building industry is called a backhoe loader. Its long arm and bucket at the back can reach and dig. Its front bucket can scoop and lift. It can be used in road building, snow clearing, demolition and mining.

loader

bucket

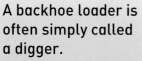

A backhoe loader is often simply called a digger.

cab

backhoe

stick

boom

rear bucket

stabilizing leg

19

Tractors at war

When countries are at war with each other, tractors can help to build defences and clear paths. They can be used to destroy buildings that have become unsafe.

Army tractors are often desert coloured.

The JCB HMEE backhoe loader has a lower cab than normal to keep the driver safe.

21

Mega tractors

One of the strongest production tractors in the world is the Steiger Quadtrac 620. It has enormous crawler wheels to spread its weight over the ground and make it go faster.

The Valtra T234 tractor holds the record for the world's fastest tractor.

FACT...

The largest farm tractor in the world is the Big Bud 747. It is 4.25 metres tall and each of its tyres measures 2.4 metres across.

SPOTLIGHT: *Steiger Quadtrac 620*

Famous for:	one of the strongest tractors
Built by:	Case IH
Built:	2014
Engine power:	683 horsepower

Future tractors

So what next for tractors? Will farmers soon be using robot tractors? Driverless tractors can work alongside a farmer, and even through the night, if they are programmed correctly.

Driverless tractors use GPS (Global Positioning System) technology to carry out jobs on a farm.

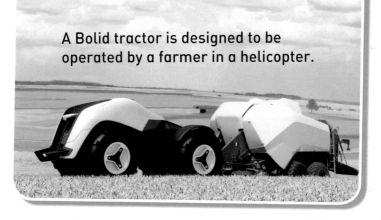

A Bolid tractor is designed to be operated by a farmer in a helicopter.

FACT...

The manufacturer John Deere tried to develop a walking tractor that could travel down mountains and through mud. The design was abandoned.

What will farm tractors look like in the future?

Dancing tractors

It takes great skill to drive a tractor over bumpy ground without tipping it backwards or onto its side. And it takes great skill to make a tractor dance! But that is what some tractor drivers do to entertain people at agricultural shows.

Square dancing tractors dance in formation.

FACT...

The JCB Dancing Diggers pass each other
with only centimetres to spare.

The drivers of the JCB Dancing Diggers
perform a 'handstand'.

Tractor pulls

Which is the most powerful motor sport that uses wheeled vehicles? Motorbike racing? No. Sports car racing? No. Tractor pulling? Yes! At a tractor pulling competition, powerful tractors fitted with extra engines pull a very heavy sled along a 100-metre track.

FACT...

Adapted tractors at a tractor pulling competition can have an engine strength of 10,000 horsepower. That's the same as the strength of 10,000 horses!

This tractor is called Baby Duck. It is modified each year and has won several European championships.

GLOSSARY

agricultural Anything to do with farming.

attachments Mechanical items that can be hooked onto a tractor.

combustion engine An engine that burns fuel to power a machine.

concrete A building material made of sand, stones and cement.

crawler wheels Wheels that run inside a metal loop. They have a better grip than normal wheels.

defences Structures that are built to protect people or buildings.

demolition Knocking something down.

diesel engine An engine that burns diesel fuel to power a machine.

excavator A huge tractor with an enormous bucket for digging and moving earth or rocks.

grain The nut-like part of a cereal crop.

grapples Hand-like grips that are attached to a long tractor arm.

hydraulic hitch A lifting mechanism that positions an attachment at the height required by the farmer for the job.

plough A series of discs and blades that break up soil ready for planting.

stabilizing Stopping something from giving way or falling over.

stalk The stem of a plant.

traction engine A road vehicle that is used to pull very heavy loads. Traction engines are powered by either steam or diesel fuel.

trailer A wheeled cart that can be pulled behind a vehicle.

treads The raised parts of a tyre.

vehicle A machine that can move and take people or things from place to place. Cars, trucks, buses and tractors are vehicles.

INDEX

Collect all the titles in this series!

BEASTLY
BUGS
FREE Collector Cards and Downloadable Audio!

DEADLY
DINOSAURS
FREE Collector Cards and Downloadable Audio!

FANTASTIC
FLIERS
FREE Collector Cards and Downloadable Audio!

FAST
CARS
FREE Collector Cards and Downloadable Audio!

FREEZING
POLES
FREE Collector Cards and Downloadable Audio!

MIGHTY
TRUCKS
FREE Collector Cards and Downloadable Audio!

RIOTOUS
RAINFORESTS
FREE Collector Cards and Downloadable Audio!

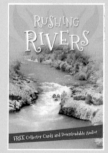

RUSHING
RIVERS
FREE Collector Cards and Downloadable Audio!